RENEWAL

Ray and Anne Ortlund

NAVPRESS

A MINISTRY OF THE NAVIGATORS
P.O. BOX 6000, COLORADO SPRINGS, COLORADO 80934

The Navigators is an international Christian organization. Jesus Christ gave His followers the Great Commission to go and make disciples (Matthew 28:19). The aim of The Navigators is to help fulfill that commission by multiplying laborers for Christ in every nation.

NavPress is the publishing ministry of The Navigators. NavPress publications are tools to help Christians grow. Although publications alone cannot make disciples or change lives, they can help believers learn biblical discipleship, and apply what they learn to their lives and ministries.

© 1989 by Raymond C. and Anne Ortlund
All rights reserved, including translation
ISBN 08910-95462

Cover photography: Mark Reis

Material in this study guide is adapted from *Lord, Make My Life a Miracle* by Raymond C. Ortlund (Regal Books, 1974); *Three Priorities for a Strong Local Church* by Raymond C. Ortlund (Word, Inc., 1983, 1988); *Disciplines of the Beautiful Woman* by Anne Ortlund (Word, Inc., 1977, 1984); *Be a New Christian All Your Life* by Raymond C. Ortlund (Fleming H. Revell, 1983); and *Discipling One Another* by Anne Ortlund (Word, Inc., 1979, 1984).

All Scripture quotations in this publication are from the *Holy Bible: New International Version*. Copyright © 1973, 1978, 1984, International Bible Society. Used by permission of Zondervan Bible Publishers.

Printed in the United States of America

FOR A FREE CATALOG OF
NAVPRESS BOOKS & BIBLE STUDIES,
CALL TOLL FREE 800-366-7788 (USA)
or 1-416-499-4615 (CANADA)

Contents

Authors

Through their speaking and writing, Ray and Anne Ortlund have touched thousands of people on every continent. For twenty years their ministry was centered in Pasadena, California, where Ray was pastor of the Lake Avenue Congregational Church. They are now involved in Renewal Ministries, a unique ministry based in Newport Beach, California.

Ray Ortlund, a graduate of the University of Puget Sound and Princeton Theological Seminary, has also been honored by Talbot Theological Seminary with the Doctor of Divinity degree. He is the author of *Lord, Make My Life a Miracle* and *Lord, Make My Life Count*.

Anne Ortlund is particularly well-known as a speaker at women's conferences. In addition, she is an organist and composer, having penned more than 250 songs and hymns including the award-winning "Macedonia." Her previous books include *Disciplines of the Beautiful Woman* and *Children Are Wet Cement*.

How to Use This Study Guide

Anybody can study renewal and go away unchanged. Our desire for you as you use this guide is not just to study renewal, but to be renewed. That's why you will spend as much or more time practicing renewal as talking about it.

This guide is designed to be used in a group of four to eight people. If your group contains more than eight people, you can stay together for worship, but divide into groups of three or four for discussion and "Moving Out" exercises. It's important that everyone have a chance to respond to all of the questions, and this won't be possible in groups of more than eight people. (Shy people won't talk, and you'll run out of time.) Don't worry if some discussion groups don't have a trained leader. Just choose someone to keep the group moving and away from tangents.

Sessions 1-8 contain the following:

▶an adapted excerpt from one or more of the Ortlunds' books;
▶a warm-up exercise to help you grow closer together as a group;
▶questions to explore what the Bible says about the topic at hand;
▶questions that will enable you to share what you each

think and feel about the topic;
▶exercises for putting the topic into practice together;
▶homework for putting it into practice during the week.

You don't need to come to group meetings having looked at the scriptures or answered the questions on paper. However, it's essential that you come having read the book excerpt for the session and done the homework.

The homework mainly consists of spending twenty minutes a day with God and talking on the telephone with one other group member. If you're faithful in these disciplines, by the end of the study series you'll have made a habit of them. As you'll discover, they will become the essential building blocks of renewal in your life. So don't think of them as homework; think of them as a chance to practice—with the support of fellow learners—some habits that will enrich the rest of your life.

Try to allow one and a half to two hours for each group meeting. You'll be rushed in less than ninety minutes. If you have a talkative group, plan more time or carefully select which questions to cover. Don't run out of time to do the group exercises at the end.

As Anne says in session 4, worship should be a part of a balanced group meeting. Worship helps to draw our attention away from ourselves and our circumstances, and draws us toward the God who can do something about them. Plan fifteen minutes toward the beginning of your meetings for worship. You might sing a few songs or hymns, read a psalm or two aloud together—whatever means "worship" for your group.

Only God can renew a life. So, as you work through this study, keep asking Him to help you not only learn His truth, but also work it out in your daily life. Expect Him to begin a fresh work in your life as you study and apply His living Word.

*We must be the people of God before we do
the work of God.*
—Ray & Anne Ortlund

What Are My Priorities?

The large California church I was pastoring seemed fine.
Visitors would murmur all the right words about "great
missionary emphasis" and "great youth program." But
my heart wasn't satisfied. There were too few "delivery-
room" cries of newborns, too few victory songs at
midnight.

I had exclaimed in anguish many times in my life,
"I refuse to be an ordinary Christian!"

Then I read a sentence from Thomas Kelly that set
my heart on fire. He prayed, "Lord, make my life a
miracle."

*Oh, God! That's it! You're the original Miracle, and I
live in You. Why shouldn't my life be a miracle? Why
shouldn't I be able to show others how to be miracles?*

I gathered some close brothers and sisters around to
pray and brainstorm. I asked, "What are the biblical
priorities? What are the basics that are absolutely rock-
bottom—whether in the year two hundred AD or two
thousand AD?"

At the early church service six weeks later, I said to
our people, "I have a plan. We need to turn a new corner.
We need a fresh start. Would you join me in three commitments? I'll be the first to sign my name.

9

"Number one: At whatever stage you are spiritually, commit your heart anew to the Person of God Himself in Jesus Christ.

"Number two: Commit yourself to the Body of Christ, to be in a regular small group of believers, small enough so that you can be personally accountable to them for your growth and personally responsible for their growth.

"Number three: Commit yourself to the world, to your work in it and your witness to it. Make your commitment specific enough to vow to love one person to Jesus by next Easter.

"If you're willing to commit yourself to these three priorities in this order, sign your name to it on the registration card." Six hundred people signed. We called them "The Company of the Committed," and they revolutionized our church.

What does God do through the little act of people putting their names on white cards? The act seems like nothing. But then, so does piling up a heap of stones, or killing a lamb for sacrifice. Joining the Company of the Committed represents the most exciting concept I know. It can change your life, as it has changed Anne's and mine. It says, "My three life priorities are going to be

1. God;
2. Believers;
3. My work in this world.
In that order!"

These three priorities must be kept in order. We must not let our ministry to the world—our evangelism and good works—become of first importance. We must not let our fellowship and intrachurch functioning be first. To the extent that priority three becomes priority one—or priority two comes first—we will be out of kilter, out of God's plan, and we'll become fussing, uptight, confused, and tired.

These three commitments are not hatched out of human brains. Any manmade list of priorities would be sure to stress whatever happened to be weak in a particular culture at that certain period of time. No, these three priorities shine repeatedly from the pages of Scripture. They are deeply, fundamentally planted in the heart of God.[1]

Warm-up

If your group members are new to each other, it will be invaluable to spend a little time at each meeting getting to know each other. One way to do this is with a life profile. For the first meeting, let the group leader come prepared to share his or her profile. Then let someone else come with a profile to share at each succeeding meeting. (If your group has more than eight people, share two profiles at each meeting.) It shouldn't take more than five or ten minutes to share a profile.

A life profile is a graph that starts at your birth and goes to the present, charting your spiritual, emotional, and physical ups and downs. It might look something like this:

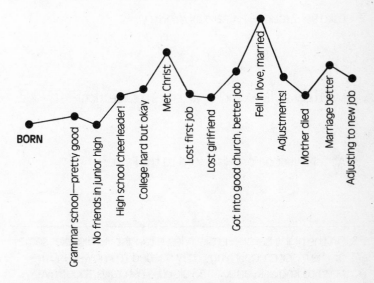

When the person is finished explaining his or her profile briefly, the group can pray one-sentence prayers of thanks or petition for where the person has been and is now.

Scripture Search

Ray says that the three priorities he's listed "are deeply, fundamentally planted in the heart of God." Study the following scriptures to see if you agree.

---

1. Read Matthew 22:34-40 aloud. According to Jesus, what should be a person's first and second priorities?

---

2. When He returned to the Father, Jesus left His disciples with a third priority. He stated it several times in different ways. What does He say about that priority in the following passages?

   Luke 9:1-2 (during His earthly ministry)

   Matthew 28:18-20 (shortly after His resurrection)

   Acts 1:8 (just before His return to the Father)

---

3. On the night before He died, Jesus taught His disciples some of the most crucial things they needed to know—and we need to know. Read John 15 aloud. Then take about five minutes to examine this chapter for the three priorities and jot notes in the following chart. Then discuss: "What does Jesus say about these life priorities?"

"Abide in Christ" (John 15:1-11).

"Love each other" (John 15:12-17).

"Testify to the world" (John 15:18-27).

Optional: Later that evening, Jesus prayed His heart's desire to the Father (John 17). He seemed to have three basic areas of concern. If you're not convinced yet that the three priorities are biblical, explore the following questions:

a. What was Jesus' first priority in His prayer (17:1-5)? What did He ask for?

b. How does this priority apply to us?

c. What is Jesus' second priority (17:6-19)? What are some of the things He asked for?

d. How can this be our concern?

e. What is Jesus' focus in 17:20-26? (See especially verses 21-23.)

f. What seems to be our part in giving ourselves to this third priority?

If you're still not convinced, take a look at Colossians 1:15-20 (first priority), 2:1–4:1 (second priority), and 4:2-6 (third priority).

---

4. a. What is the connection between glorifying Christ and loving His people (John 14:23-24, 15:9-17)?

b. According to John 13:35 and 17:21-23, what is the connection between loving other Christians and testifying to the world that Jesus is the Savior?

c. How does reaching out to a lost world with the gospel show love for Christ?

Moving Out

---

5. a. What practical steps would it take for you to make abiding in and glorifing Christ your first priority?

b. What would it cost you to make this your first priority?

c. What would be the benefits?

---

6. a. What would your life look like if other Christians were your second priority?

b. What are the risks involved in doing this?

c. What are the potential benefits?

---

7. a. What might your part be in giving yourself to the third priority?

b. What, if anything, makes you uncomfortable about accepting this priority?

8. Take a look at your checkbook and your calendar. (Review them in your mind if you don't have them with you.) What do the ways you spend your time and money reveal about your personal priorities?

9. Christians too often arrange their priorities for living based on their personal circumstances or our present culture, rather than on what seem to be the top areas of biblical concern. If you were to base your first three life priorities on your own circumstances or your culture—just from human reasoning—what might your priorities be?

If you agree that the three priorities we've named are biblical, commit yourselves as a group to making them the first, second, and third priorities of your lives. Do this verbally, and give everyone in the group a chance to voice hesitations. You aren't giving each other blanket permission to interfere in your lives, but you are giving God permission to begin teaching you what these priorities mean and how He wants them to affect you. It's scary to invite God to move, but it's worth it!

10. In the next seven sessions you'll have a chance to explore how these priorities can set your personal lives, your families, your group, and your church on a firm foundation. For now, take this short self-inventory:

    a. Which of the three priorities do you think you are strongest in? Why?

b. Which do you think you are weakest in, and why?

c. Ask God what one goal He would like you to set for your-self as you explore the three priorities for the next eight weeks. Think and pray about this for a few minutes, then write down your goal. (If you can think of lots of goals, write down no more than three.)

My goal(s) for this study series:

Pray together for God to begin ordering your lives according to His priorities. Thank Him for what He has already done for each of you in this area. Pray specifically for each person in your group regarding the priority he or she identified as weakest.

Other Voices
Every person really needs three conversions—to Christ, to the Church, and to the world.[2]

—Stephen Neill

The Relationship of the Believers with Jesus (John 15:1-11). *The first and most important relationship which the disciples should maintain was with Jesus. . . .*
    The Relationship of Believers to Each Other (John 15:12-17). *Having explained the essential relationship of believers to Himself, Jesus proceeded to show His disciples what their relationship to each other should be. . . .*
    The Relationship of Believers to the World (John

15:18-27). *The third relation which the believer must maintain is with the world. Jesus never intended that he should live in pious isolation, but in active contact with the problems of men.*[3]

—Merrill C. Tenney

For the Group Leader

You may not be able to cover all of the questions in this session. You can skip question 4 if time is short. You can save questions 5 through 7 for later sessions, when you will be exploring the three priorities in more detail. But don't rush into commitment to the priorities out of peer pressure. Give everyone a chance to say why he is or isn't prepared to accept each of the priorities for himself, and to make his own decision.

NOTES
1. Adapted from Raymond C. Ortlund, *Lord, Make My Life a Miracle* (Ventura, Calif.: Regal Books, 1974), pages 1-4; and Raymond C. Ortlund, *Three Priorities for a Strong Local Church* (Waco, Tex.: Word Books, 1983, 1988), pages 17-19.
2. Stephen Neill, *The Unfinished Task* (London: Edinburgh House Press, 1957), page 67.
3. Merrill C. Tenney, *John: The Gospel of Belief* (Grand Rapids, Mich.: Eerdmans, 1948), pages 226-230.

PRIORITY ONE
Christ

*Sin will keep you from His presence, or His
presence will keep you from sin.*
                    —*Ray & Anne Ortlund*

Practicing God's Presence

Thomas Kelly, a recent Quaker, wrote,

> We are unhappy, uneasy, strained, oppressed, and
> fearful we shall be shallow.
>   Over the margins of life comes a whisper, a faint
> call, a premonition of richer living which we know we
> are passing by. . . . We have hints that there is a way
> of life vastly richer and deeper than all this hurried
> existence, a life of unhurried serenity and peace and
> power.
>   If only we could slip over into that Center! If only
> we could find the Silence which is the source of
> sound![1]

One summer vacation I stumbled onto the writings of
Thomas Kelly. I had always believed in the centrality of
God; I had taught the doctrine of it. But I wasn't living it.
    You see, today we are activists. We love Christ, but we
don't stay much around Him. We talk gladly of God's for-
giveness, but we don't have too much time to wait on
God, or for God, or with God. We are on the move. We run
into prayer, and then we say, "I've got to get on with life,
on with real life."

How unaware we are of what "the real" really is!

God calls us to live *with Him.* This is not the idea of the omnipresence of God. It isn't the idea that I invited Jesus to come into my heart. Those are wonderful, but they're not what I'm talking about. I'm talking about consciously, continually living in the presence of God. Going in and out and finding pasture, as it were. Speaking with Him, talking with Him, enjoying Him, loving Him—rejoicing, praising, crying, complaining—all those things, in the presence of God.

Augustus Strong's *Systematic Theology* says, "The majority of Christians much more frequently think of Christ as a Saviour *outside of them* than as a Saviour who dwells within."

We think of Christ as in Heaven, 'way up there.

Now, here is our desk with a pile of papers we are trying to go through, while the phone is ringing off the hook.

Or the kitchen has to be cleaned, and somebody has just spilled orange juice on the floor, and we've got to go get groceries.

Or we're in a classroom, and there's a paper due tomorrow morning or it's one point off our grade.

There are so many immediate *now* problems, and they get first "dibs" on our attention because we *think they're closest!* We haven't yet learned that "in him we live and move and have our being" (Acts 17:28). We don't understand that He is closer than our problems! We haven't yet learned to *live from the inside out.*[2]

Warm-up
Take five or ten minutes to let one group member share his or her life profile. Then pray briefly for that person.

Scripture Search

1. Ray says, "Today we are activists." Would you say this is true of you? Why or why not?

2. Read Psalm 62 aloud.

  a. From what little he says about them, what seem to be David's circumstances as he writes this song?

  b. How does he decide to deal with his circumstances?

  c. Make a list of everything David says in this psalm about how he relates to God, and God to him.

3. David says, "My soul finds rest in God alone" (Psalm 62:1). On a scale of 1 to 10, how much at rest would you say your soul is today? (Circle your answer.)

  1   2   3   4   5   6   7   8   9   10

4. Now, on a scale of 1 to 10, to what extent have you spent time in the past twenty-four hours aware of and focused on God's presence with you?

  1   2   3   4   5   6   7   8   9   10

5. a. What are some of the things (circumstances, attitudes, memories, priorities) that hinder you from finding rest in God alone?

b. What can you do to overcome those hindrances?

6. Read John 15:1-6 aloud. What do you think it means, in practical terms, to "remain" or "abide" in Christ?

THINK ABOUT IT: Do you really believe that apart from Jesus
you can do *nothing* (John 15:5)? Do your actions show it?

7. Read aloud John 15:9-10. How will you feel if you consciously,
moment by moment, abide in Christ's love? What will
happen to your worries and fears?

Are you saying, "I'm really afraid of total surrender; I've got
so many dreams and plans, and I'm not sure what would
happen to them if I gave myself totally to God"?

The first Queen Elizabeth asked a man to go abroad for
her on business.

"I sincerely wish I could, but I can't," said the man. "My
business is very demanding. It would really suffer if I left."

"Sir," replied the Queen, "if you will attend to *my* business, I will take care of *your* business."[3]

—Anne Ortlund

8. a. Which aspect of your "business" (if any) are you most afraid God might not take care of if you gave yourself totally to Him?

   b. How sensible do you really think your fear is? Why?

9. a. It is common for Christians to pray, "Lord, be with me [or Fred or Mary] today in this situation." But what do Jesus and the Father promise in the following passages?

   Matthew 28:20

   Hebrews 13:5

   b. How do you think this promise should affect the way you live your life?

Moving Out
Choose one or both of the following group exercises (questions 10 and 11), as well as the homework assignment (question 12).

10. Take three minutes right now to write a four-line psalm of praise to the Lord. Express whatever you are feeling or thinking about Him. Write your psalm *to Him* to give Him pleasure from you personally. It can rhyme, but it doesn't have to; it can be blank verse, or you can try the parallelism you find in the biblical psalms.

After the three minutes are up, the leader can ask those in the group who are willing to do so to read what they wrote. (Some may not care to read theirs.) The point is not to show off but to represent the rest of the group in an act of group worship. Suggest that the other group members be in the attitude of "Amen," "Lord, I agree," "That's from me too."

---

11. Break up into groups of two. Spend ten minutes taking turns just talking aloud to God. Tell Him how your day went, how you feel about Him, how you feel about other things—whatever seems important. Try to avoid "churchy" language; instead, talk to God as if He were a Person (because He is). If it helps, imagine that you and your partner and God are sitting together over coffee or on the phone. Don't pray for yourselves or other people; just discuss with God what's going on with you.

After ten minutes, take stock of your own heart. If you feel that some attitude or circumstance in your life is hindering you from putting God first, tell Him about that and ask Him to deal with it. Ask Him to enable you to remain in Him this week.

When you have finished talking to God, take a couple of minutes to discuss how you felt while you were doing it. Was it easy or awkward? Why?

12. a. During the next week, take ten or fifteen minutes each day to just talk with God (see question 11). Set a time four days from now when each of you will telephone one other person in your group to see how that prayer time has been. Your job is to gently keep each other accountable and to give each other a chance to share joys, frustrations, and needs.

b. Copy the promise in Hebrews 13:5 or a verse from Psalm 62 onto a piece of paper. Tape it where you will see it several times a day (on your refrigerator, your desk, your dashboard). Each time you see it, thank God that what the verse says is true. Try to memorize the verse, and remind yourself of God's presence at other times during the day.

Other Voices

The old saying of "putting first things first" is not quite good enough. The New Testament makes it evident that the "first" of which it speaks is singular and not plural; "putting the first thing first" would be the only proper statement of the matter. . . . Anything else that might be taken out of "all the rest" and set up as "first" inevitably will result in doublemindedness rather than a single focus.[4]

—Vernard Eller

For me the time of action does not differ from the time of prayer, and in the noise and clatter of my kitchen, while several persons are calling for as many different things, I possess God in as great tranquility as upon my knees.[5]

—Brother Lawrence

For the Group Leader

Be sure to keep the sharing of life profiles to no more than ten minutes. It should take about sixty minutes to discuss questions 1 through 9, and you'll need fifteen minutes to do either question 10 or 11. If necessary, omit one or more of questions 1

through 9. Don't spend so much time talking that there isn't
enough time to put what you've said into action!

NOTES
1. Thomas Kelly, *A Testament of Devotion* (New York: Harper and Brothers,
   1941), page 115.
2. Adapted from Raymond C. Ortlund, *Lord, Make My Life a Miracle* (Ventura,
   Calif.: Regal Books, 1974), pages 9-13.
3. Anne Ortlund, *Disciplines of the Beautiful Woman* (Waco, Tex.: Word, Inc.,
   1977, 1984), page 25.
4. Vernard Eller, *The Simple Life* (Grand Rapids, Mich.: Eerdmans, 1973), page 21.
5. Brother Lawrence, *The Practice of the Presence of God* (Old Tappan, N.J.:
   Fleming H. Revell, 1985), page IV.

*Is God really Number One in your life?
Show me your checkbook and your
calendar.*
                                        —Ray Ortlund

Thirsting for God Daily

There is one prime, basic, all-important place in your life
where the rubber really meets the road. At this place, my
friend, you win or lose—you make it or you don't.

The place I'm talking about is where you go down on
your knees, where you shut out all the rest of the world,
and you and God—just the two of you—get together.

It has to be honest between you and Him.

It has to be regular, at least once a day.

And it has to be fought for, clawed and scratched
for—or it will never happen.

As sweet as life is in practicing God's presence, that
doesn't rule out your need for a consistent encounter
where it's just God and you.

George Mueller, the man of great faith in nineteenth-
century England, shared his reason for spiritual power:

> The first thing to be concerned about was not how
> much I might serve the Lord, but how I might get my
> soul into a happy state, and how my inner man
> might be nourished. . . .
>
> I began therefore to meditate on the New Testa-
> ment from the beginning, early in the morning. The
> first thing I did, after having asked in a few words

29

the Lord's blessing upon His precious Word, was to begin to meditate on the Word of God, searching out of it, not for the sake of public ministry of the Word, not for the sake of preaching on what I had meditated upon, but for obtaining for my own soul.[1]

You don't get food for your soul by osmosis! You can hear others talk of it; but until you regularly take in the delicious Word of God, you're undernourished.

It was important for Christ. That in itself should make us go after quiet times with God. Think of it. Jesus withdrew for long periods of time to be alone with His Father.

"Very early in the morning, while it was still dark, Jesus got up, left the house and went off to a solitary place, where he prayed" (Mark 1:35). Evidently even the eternal Christ needed quiet periods of prayer: "Jesus often withdrew to lonely places and prayed" (Luke 5:16).

It is not easy for us to understand, of course. Jesus was the Son of God; why was it necessary? He was "with God"; He "was God" (John 1:1). Jesus practiced the presence of God in an utter and complete way. Yet He still got away for deliberate prayer. He shut out the world for large hunks of time and communicated with His Father.

You may say, "But Jesus didn't live in the twentieth century!" My friend, we all have time for what we really want.

Choose a quiet place and a particular time for this daily tryst. Anytime becomes no time. Fix a daily appointment with God. Write it in your date book!

If I sound like the professional who's had all this mastered for years, let me tell you, Ray Ortlund sweats it out. There are plenty of pressures on my time. Through the years I've wavered back and forth between frustration and success.

Whenever you and God are to meet together is up to you and Him. Let me warn you though: when you can't or you fail to meet your appointment, don't beat yourself for it. After all, who are you to think you can be so perfect or consistent? And who am I? But by His strength, keep at it!

The goal of your Bible reading can be reached by asking yourself the same two questions that Paul asked on the Damascus road (Acts 22:8,10):

> "Who are You, Lord?" (Write down all that you learn about Him.)
> "What shall I do, Lord?" (Write down how you can obey what you've read.)

In that holy time before the Book, have a double goal: to know God, and to obey Him.[2]

Warm-up
Take five or ten minutes to let one group member share his or her life profile, then pray for that person briefly.

---

1. What reasons does Ray give for having a daily time with God?

---

2. In session 2, you committed yourselves to spending ten minutes each day talking to God about your lives.

   a. How did it go?

   b. What obstacles, if any, got in the way of your doing this?

   c. How did the experience affect you?

Scripture Search

3. Read Psalm 63 aloud.

   a. How does David feel about God?

   b. How does he express those feelings in actions?

---

4. Anne says, "A thirst for God is normal living, like thirst for liquids. A lack of thirst for God is shocking, abnormal, a sign of spiritual sickness or deadness."

   a. Do you agree with this? Why or why not?

   b. Are you thirsty for God? If so, what drives you to that thirst? If not, what do you think is preventing that thirst?

   c. What can a person do to become more aware of his or her natural thirst for God?

5. How does David describe the way he seeks God in the following psalms?

Psalm 130

Psalm 131

6. What do you think it means to wait for the Lord more than watchmen wait for the morning (Psalm 130:6)?

7. a. Why is a still, childlike soul (Psalm 131:2) important in seeking the Lord?

b. How does a person go about quieting his soul?

8. As a group, brainstorm a list of all the reasons why you are inclined *not* to bother to schedule daily time with God. Write them down even if you know they're false or selfish reasons suggested by our spiritual enemy. (Be honest! If you're not all having time with God each day, you must have some reasons why!)

Moving Out

We're all busy. The difference between the people who will do *anything* to protect their daily time with God and those who won't is that the first group is *enthralled* by the majesty and love of the God they seek. The following exercises are intended to help you become enthralled!

Choose one or more of the group exercises (questions 9 through 12), as well as the homework assignment (question 13).

9. Many religious and psychological theories advocate quieting your mind and meditating, but biblical Christianity calls us to still our thoughts in order to focus on Jesus Christ and His Father.

Who is this God we serve? Assign each of the following passages to a different member of the group. Have those people read their passages aloud in turn. Ask them to read with expression, in praise to God.

▶ Exodus 34:5-8
▶ Isaiah 9:6-7
▶ Colossians 1:13-20
▶ Revelation 5:6-14

After all of the passages have been read, take ten minutes to sit silently and worship the God you've been hearing about. Quiet your souls, and wait on God with earnest expectation. Enjoy His presence, as a child with his mother would. Don't tell God things or ask Him for anything; just focus on Him. If your mind starts buzzing with activity, draw it back to stillness. If your mind wanders, spend part of your time writing your thoughts to God—yet spend time listening as well as writing. Don't reprimand yourself for wandering to other thoughts; just go back to focusing on God.

When you are finished, take about five minutes to let group members describe what they experienced during this silent time. What did the scriptures impress upon you about God? Did they touch your hearts in any areas of your lives?

---

10. Read Colossians 1:15-20. In a group of three or four, discuss what this passage says about Christ. Then spend about ten minutes writing praise and adoration to Christ for who He is and what He has done for you. Don't worry if you're not a great communicator; just write what you feel toward Jesus. Let the leader end this by leading the whole group in singing the Doxology or some other worship song that everyone knows without books.

11. Take ten minutes to worship the Lord with short sentence prayers using this formula: "Lord, You are . . . ." (For instance: "Lord, You are eternal." "Lord, You are my Good Shepherd.") Don't pray around the circle, but back and forth, in and out. Each of you may pray many times, but just one sentence at a time. (One-sentence worship prayers would also be a good response to the readings in question 9 as an alternative to silent worship.)

12. Jesus Christ is the Alpha and the Omega, everything from A to Z. In worship, praise Him by calling out one-word attributes and names that begin with "A" (Almighty, etc.), then "B," and so on.

13. Divide into pairs (not the same pairs as last time). Discuss whether you want to commit yourselves to spending time with God daily. Explain your reasons for your decision.

    If you decide that the pros outweigh the cons, take five minutes to help each other plan times when you can each spend at least twenty minutes in prayer and Bible reading daily. One of you may decide to do it before breakfast, while the other may have less hurried time at noon. Agree that one of you will telephone the other during the coming week so that you can compare notes on how things are going.

    Spend ten minutes of your time each day reading a chapter of Paul's letter to the Philippians, and then writing what you learn from these questions (Acts 22:8,10):

"Who are You, Lord?"
"What should I do, Lord?"

Each day, write down what you see about the Lord in the passage ("Who are You, Lord?") and how you can obey the passage in your own life ("What should I do, Lord?"). If you do this every day for a week, you'll get through Philippians almost twice.

Spend the other ten minutes each day talking to God.
To keep your mind focused, speak aloud or write prayers
using the following "ACTS" formula:

▶ two minutes: **A**doration (tell Him about Himself!)
▶ two minutes: **C**onfession of your sins (1 John 1:9)
▶ three minutes: **T**hanksgiving for specific blessings
▶ three minutes: **S**upplication (strong, specific requests
of a great God!)

Other Voices

*When our three babies were age 2½, 1½, and brand
new, I found my days were just one succession of
bottles and diapers, and I got desperate for times with
the Lord! Normally I sleep like a rock, but I said, "Lord,
if you'll help me, I'll meet you from two to three A.M." I
kept my tryst with him until the schedule lightened;
I didn't die; and I'm not sorry I did it. Everybody has
twenty-four hours. We can soak ourselves in prayer, in
his Word, in himself, if we really want to.[3]*

—Anne Ortlund

*Believers may not often realize it, but even as believers
we are either centered on man, or centered on God.
There is no alternative. Either God is the center of our
universe and we have become rightly adjusted to him,
or we have made ourselves the center and are attempt-
ing to make all else orbit around us and for us.[4]*

—DeVern F. Fromke

NOTES
1. V. Raymond Edman, *Devotions Are a Delight* (Oradell, N.J.: American Tract Society).
2. Adapted from Raymond C. Ortlund, *Lord, Make My Life a Miracle* (Ventura, Calif.: Regal Books, 1974), pages 31-35.
3. Anne Ortlund, *Disciplines of the Beautiful Woman* (Waco, Tex.: Word, Inc., 1977, 1984), page 25.
4. DeVern F. Fromke, *Ultimate Intention* (Mount Vernon, Mo.: Sure Foundation Publishers, 1962), page 10.

PRIORITY TWO
The Body of Christ

When God came down to this planet, He didn't stand across the street and shout through a megaphone, "I love you!" He chose a small group and got with them eyeball to eyeball, to show that godly love is intimate love.

—Ray & Anne Ortlund

Nurture in Small Groups

When it is honest, open, and loving at intimate levels, Christianity powerfully changes human behavior.

Any local church is a gathering of people with many, many wounds. They come out of a world where they've been beaten up from one week to the next. They need grace, love, and tender handling, and they need it from each other. Small groups give us the perfect opportunity to be "unshockable, democratic, permissive" (as Bruce Larson says)—to be comforting, to be "shock absorbers."

But more than that is needed. Christians who are unshockable and loving are the only ones qualified to also be corrective. People going through temptations and difficult times especially need the loving closeness of a few brothers and sisters who will hold them accountable.

+ + +

In a small group of peers the idea is, "Where you're strong and I'm weak, you'll help me. Where I'm strong and you're weak, I'll help you. We'll all learn about Jesus from each other."

How often do you meet? Well, you meet together regularly, probably weekly, although I know many teenagers and businessmen who also check in by telephone daily.

41

Have the feeling, though, that this is not a meeting; it's
a relationship. That means you're on call twenty-four
hours a day, seven days a week.

We've found by trial and error that groups can be
four to eight people. With more than eight you can begin
to become anonymous; there's not time for the quiet ones
to share their lives.

The meeting time must be systematic and struc-
tured so that it doesn't turn into a coffee klatch. Four
people will probably need one to one and a half hours
weekly together; I'm in a group of four that needs two.
Our group of eight last year found we needed two full
hours, without including time for food; even then we
barely made it.

This is not a Bible study, but it must include God's
Word—enough of it for your life situations to spring out
of it. It's not primarily for information. Your adult Sunday school classes and other Bible classes provide that.

This is not a prayer meeting, but it must include
prayer—sometimes more, sometimes less. Vary the pat-
tern; vary the format for freshness.

This is not a worship service, but it must include
worship. Every time you gather in Jesus' name, spend
part of your time focusing on Him alone. You may worship Him in prayer. You may sing to Him, or read
together the words of worship hymns. You may pray
psalms to Him, or talk of His attributes. Use your sancti-
fied ingenuity!

This is not a sensitivity group, but it must include
sharing. Don't let the sharing swallow up the whole time!
Sharing should not often come first; we all are too prone
to forget about the time when we talk about ourselves.
Still, sharing is a crucial part and needs special con-
sideration.

Some people are afraid to get into small groups
because they fear getting trapped into a confession session. Boy, so do I! Is it "airing dirty linen"? Count me out!
And yet, with hundreds of small groups in our church
over many years, I've never heard this mentioned as a

problem. You see, when you meet *in Jesus' name*, He is in the midst! And His Holy Spirit is a gentleman! When He is in charge, everything will be seemly and proper. Your group is not to be problem-centered, but Christ-centered.

Plenty of things will never be exposed. There are things in my past I wouldn't tell anybody. Why should I? God has forgiven and forgotten them. Yet there will be times when you need your brothers and sisters to help you over a temptation or sin, and that's exactly what a small group is for. The point of a small group is to lift, to encourage, to edify, to "strengthen one another in God," as Jonathan did David.

The last essential ingredient is accountability for and responsibility to each other. Setting and sharing goals helps here. If you know your brother or sister's highest dreams and longings, you know him or her better, and you know how to pray for that person. And when he knows your dreams and longings, you have put yourself on the line to be accountable. As a functioning member of the Body, he should say to you from time to time, "How are you doing? How is your quiet time coming? Have you been able to witness to your neighbor?" Submission to the Body of Christ includes vulnerability, but that's what moves us all along faster in our spiritual progress.[1]

Warm-up
Let someone share his or her life profile for five or ten minutes. Then pray briefly for that person.

Scripture Search

1. Last week you committed yourselves to spending twenty minutes a day with God. Evaluate your experience specifically. How did it go? What happened? What did you learn from the experience?

2. You should have read Paul's letter to the Philippians at least once during the past week. Paul has a lot to say in that letter about relationships among Christians. What did you notice?

3. One instruction Paul gives is, "Each of you should look not only to your own interests, but also to the interests of others" (Philippians 2:4). The example Paul gives to explain what he means is Christ (2:5-11). How did Christ exemplify what Paul wants us to do?

THINK ABOUT IT: Jesus makes the same point in John 15:12-13 that Paul makes in Philippians 2:4-11. What does it mean, in practical terms, to lay down your (physical, emotional, spiritual) life for someone else?

4. Paul makes a related point in Galatians 6:2—"Carry each other's burdens, and in this way you will fulfill the law of Christ."

   a. What is "the law of Christ"? (Remember John 15:12-13.)

b. What do you think it means to carry someone else's burden? (Look at Galatians 6:1.)

c. While we should carry each other's burdens, Paul adds, a few sentences later, that we must also watch our own moral choices, because "each one should carry his own load" (Galatians 6:5). What is Paul saying here to balance 6:2?

5. Is it easier for you to carry someone else's burden or to let someone else carry yours? Why?

6. a. What are some of the potential pitfalls of revealing your burdens to each other and committing yourselves to carrying others' burdens?

b. How can those pitfalls be minimized?

c. It's impossible to eliminate all the risks of carrying others' burdens and revealing your own to them. Is the risk worth it to you? Why or why not?

7. We name several features we think a small group should have. What do you think about each of the following?

▶ The members are "unshockable, democratic, permissive . . . shock absorbers."
▶ "Where you're strong and I'm weak, you'll help me. Where I'm strong and you're weak, I'll help you."
▶ "This is not a meeting; it's a relationship. That means you're on call twenty-four hours a day, seven days a week."
▶ "With more than eight you can begin to become anonymous."
▶ "It's not primarily for information."
▶ It must include Bible study, prayer, worship, and sharing.
▶ It's "not to be problem-centered, but Christ-centered."
▶ Accountability for and responsibility to each other are essential.

8. *Case study:* A new believer joins your group. He is living with his girlfriend. How will you handle this situation in the first month he is with you? What about in the third month? What about in the sixth? (Some biblical passages to consider are Matthew 7:1-5, 1 Corinthians 13:4-7, Galatians 6:1-5.)

Moving Out

As you have discovered, you are not just *studying* three priorities—you are also doing them! In this session, you are studying small groups—*in a small group!* Continue to pray that throughout this course, you won't just be studying how Christians get renewal, you will experience renewal in your personal lives and as a group.

Choose one or more of the following group exercises (questions 9 through 12), as well as the homework assignment (questions 13-15).

---

9. Divide into groups of three or four. Let every person in each group share one burden (a decision, a moral choice, a temptation, a trying situation, a concern) that he or she would like the rest of the group to carry during the coming week. Then discuss how the group can go about carrying that burden—in prayer for strength or guidance, in counsel, in practical help, in encouragement through a phone call.

   After each person has shared his or her burden, take five minutes to pray aloud about each one. Pray for someone else, not yourself. Just tell God your friend's situation as you understand it, and ask Him to provide the power and wisdom to handle it. Ask also that He will show you what you can do to carry that burden.

---

10. In groups of four, pray aloud for the person on your left. Avoid vague requests like, "Bless George." If you don't know what to pray for, ask the person before you pray. Holding hands is a good way of reinforcing the connections among you.

---

11. Take five minutes to prayerfully plan and write down three personal goals that you would like to achieve during the time your group is together. Make your goals as specific as possible. They can be about your time alone with God, reaching out to other believers or unbelievers, your work, your

family, your personal growth.

In a group of four, share your goals with the others. Pray for each other to attain these goals by God's empowering presence in your lives. Agree to hold each other accountable for these goals for the rest of the study sessions (or longer).

---

12. Read 1 Corinthians 13:4-8 (or Colossians 3:12-17 or 1 Thessalonians 5:12-18). Discuss how each of you would like to apply these words to your own marriage, roommate relationship, family life, church life, or friendship. As a group, brainstorm some practical ways each of you can put into practice one of the traits Paul mentions in which you feel you are imperfect. Then pray for each other to have the power—the grace from God—to do this.

---

13. Make a note of the burdens or commitments in each other's lives that you are going to pray about this week, as well as anything practical you are going to do about them. Plan to telephone one other person in your group in three or four days to find out how that person is doing. (For instance, how is he doing with the plan he set in question 12? Or, how is she dealing with the burden she expressed in question 9?)

---

14. Set aside twenty minutes each day this week to be with God. Each day, read a chapter of the book of Acts (try to get through at least chapters 1 through 6). As you read, ask yourself these questions and jot notes about any insights you get:

> ▶ How did members of the first church in Jerusalem demonstrate that Christ was number one in their lives? How is Christ exalted in this chapter of Acts?
> ▶ How did those first believers show that the Body of

Christ was their second priority? What signs of mutual love and burden-carrying do you see in this chapter?
▶What were the results of putting these two priorities first and second?
▶How do you think these priorities affected the believers' families? (See, for instance, 2:41-47; 4:4,23-37; 5:1-16; 6:1-7.)

When you've finished the chapter, spend the rest of your time talking to God about what you read, about how you are feeling and why, and especially about how much you love Him and why.

---

15. Next week, bring a copy of your upcoming week's schedule to trade with another member of your group. The schedules will give you some concrete matters to pray about for the other person each day.

Other Voices

The neighborhood bar is possibly the best counterfeit that there is to the fellowship Christ wants to give his Church. It's an imitation, dispensing liquor instead of grace, escape rather than reality—but it is a permissive, accepting, and inclusive fellowship. It is unshockable. It is democratic. You can tell people secrets, and they usually don't tell others or even want to. The bar flourishes not because most people are alcoholics, but because God has put into the human heart the desire to know and be known, to love and be loved, and so many seek a counterfeit at the price of a few beers. With all my heart, I believe that Christ wants his church to be unshockable, a fellowship where people can come in and say, I'm sunk, I'm beat, I've had it. Alcoholics Anonymous has this quality—our churches too often miss it.[2]
—Bruce Larson and Keith Miller

For the Group Leader

You don't have to cover all of the statements in question 7. Choose one or two that you think may stimulate discussion in your group. (Don't be afraid of conflict. Working through differences of opinion can bring you closer together and help you grasp God's truth more fully.)

You can use the case study in question 8 in addition to or instead of the more formal Bible study in questions 3-6. Select questions that are most likely to interest, edify, and motivate the members of your group.

Sing songs that express your oneness in Christ (such as "We Are One in the Bond of Love," "Blest Be the Tie that Binds," or "Bind Us Together, Lord").

NOTES
1. Adapted from Raymond C. Ortlund, *Three Priorities for a Strong Local Church* (Waco, Tex.: Word Books, 1983, 1988), pages 76-78; and Anne Ortlund, *Disciplines of the Beautiful Woman* (Waco, Tex.: Word, Inc., 1977, 1984), pages 85-89.
2. Bruce Larson and Keith Miller, *The Edge of Adventure* (Waco, Tex.: Word Books, 1974), page 156.

*God gives to the world the family to be the
microcosm of the Church, the mini-lab
where all His rules for living get tested.*
                                    —Anne Ortlund

Your Family as a Small Group

How wonderful it is when Christians see their families as
their primary disciples, their closest, most intimate small
group! How rich family life becomes when this is true!

If a Christian husband sees his wife and children as
just his wife and children, he'll treat them as any world-
ling does: he'll see that they're properly clothed and
schooled, marry well. . . .

But if a Christian husband sees his wife and children as his obvious, number one, built-in disciples, he'll
realize he has a limited period of time (perhaps twenty
years with each child) in which to live intimately and well
before them—so as to reproduce godliness in the next
generation. Then he will carry out Matthew 28:19 in
their lives, seeing that they are baptized and teaching
them everything Jesus has taught him. Seen in this
light, family devotions will take on fresh motivation.
Teaching loved ones to tithe, worship, have their own
quiet times, witness to the unsaved—everything will
become part of the total picture of discipling. And commitment and perseverance learned within this special
inner circle when things are rough will carry over into
the larger circle—the Church as a whole—when things
get rough there![1]

51

Warm-up

Let someone share his or her life profile for five or ten minutes. Then pray briefly for that person.

Scripture Search

---

1. a. What happened this week when you tried to carry each other's burdens in prayer and other practical ways?

   b. Which of those burdens had to do with family?

---

2. Read Ephesians 5:21–6:4. What practical guidance does God give family members for treating each other as "their closest, most intimate small group"?

   Guidance for all family members

   Guidance for wives

   Guidance for husbands

Guidance for children

Guidance for parents

---

3. Let each person answer these questions:

a. Does your family fit primarily into priority two (believers) or priority three (unbelievers)?

b. Which members fall into which category?

Moving Out

Complete questions 4 through 6. Brainstorm ideas that are as visible and measurable as possible. Help the other members in your group of four to think of plans that fit their situations. Write down all your ideas, then choose at least one from each question to begin acting on right away.

---

4. In what practical ways can you lead your family members to priority one—to love God—by modeling, verbal teaching, and things you do together?

5. In what practical ways can you lead your family members to priority two—to love the church—local, denominational, and worldwide?

6. How can you lead your family members to priority three—to love the nonChristian world?

Questions 7 and 8 are optional. If you have time, choose one according to whether your family is primarily believers (question 7) or unbelievers (question 8). Do both questions 9 and 10 as homework.

7. If your family members, spouse, or children are part of the Body of Christ, then all of the biblical commands to treat brothers and sisters in Christ with love, respect, and honor apply to the way you treat your family. They may be your kids, but they are still your spiritual brothers and sisters.

a. In what way can you carry one burden for each member of your family this week?

b. Or, how can you lay down your life for your believing family this week?

8. a. If your parents, spouse, children, or other family members are not believers, how can you set a loving example of the first two priorities that will make Christ and His Body attractive?

   b. How can you treat your family members with the kind of love Jesus showed for His unbelieving family in order to draw them to Him?

9. Divide into pairs, and commit to pray for the other person this week about the ways he wants to apply what you've discussed. Pray for grace and wisdom to include your families in your commitments to God, the Body of Christ, and the lost world. Plan to telephone each other midweek to share how it's going.

10. In your time alone with God this week, read a chapter of 2 Corinthians each day. Try to get through 1:1-6:13. Ask yourself these questions daily:

   ▶ How did Paul regard Christ?
   ▶ How did Paul regard his fellow Christians?
   ▶ What was Paul willing to go through for the sake of unbelievers?
   ▶ How should this affect my life?

For the Group Leader

Do your group's answers to question 1 reflect that families are high or low on your members' lists of concerns? Point this out after everyone has responded to question 1. In most cases, you'll find that families are of high concern.

Question 3 may be tough. It may put some group members in the position of judging their family members. To avoid this, assume that any family member who claims to be part of the Body of Christ should be treated as such. If both you and your spouse are believers, then you can treat your preteen children as part of the Body. Teenagers and adults who don't claim to be Christians belong to priority three.

The point of question 3 is to help your group see that every family member—whether or not he claims to be a Christian—fits into one of the priorities. It is also to help group members decide whether their primary task regarding their families is evangelism or discipling.

Questions 4 through 6 should be relevant whether your families are believers or unbelievers. If the latter, then your focus will be on helping them learn to love God, but you will still want to model love for both Christians and nonChristians. Love is evangelistic!

NOTE
1. Adapted from Raymond C. Ortlund, *Three Priorities for a Strong Local Church* (Waco, Tex.: Word Books, 1983, 1988), pages 80-81.

PRIORITY THREE
The World

*I want the whole Christ for my Savior, the
whole Bible for my book, the whole Church
for my fellowship, and the whole world for
my mission field.*

—John Wesley

A Heart for the Lost

Oh, how God loves people! And if He is indeed your first
priority and your heart is synchronized with His, then
you will love people too.

God has a haunting love in His heart for the world.
He forgets no one. And He wants to stretch your own
heart to share His love.

See the resurrected Christ's full-orbed vision when
the disciples asked Him, "Lord, are you at this time going
to restore the kingdom to Israel?" (Acts 1:6). Their concern was just for their own little nation. Jesus' reply was
that it was not for them to know, but then He pushed
their minds to take in larger horizons:

> "But you will receive power when the Holy Spirit
> comes on you; and you will be my witnesses in Jeru-
> salem, and in all Judea and Samaria, and to the ends
> of the earth." (Acts 1:8)

Remember when the disciples were with Jesus for a
day off, and five thousand men (how many women and
children we don't know) suddenly came storming upon
them. The Scriptures say that Jesus saw them as sheep
without a shepherd; and He had compassion on them.

59

They were guideless, leaderless, confused; and His heart was moved toward them. (See Mark 6:30-44.)

The early Christians were filled with compassion for *people*—for weary, confused people: "While they were speaking to the people" (Acts 4:1); "The apostles were teaching the people" (Acts 4:2); "The apostles performed many miraculous signs and wonders among the people" (Acts 5:12). For this the apostles were arrested and jailed, but God sent an angel and released them. Why? So that they could go back and again "tell the people the full message of this new life" (Acts 5:20)!

God loves people! And He is concerned that you love them too, that your heart stays warm and tender toward them.

F.B. Meyer, the famous British preacher, once spent a night in the home of A.B. Simpson, the founder of the Christian and Missionary Alliance. Early the next morning Mr. Meyer stole downstairs, thinking he was the first one up.

But no—through the partially open door to the study, Mr. Meyer could see Mr. Simpson in prayer. He had a world globe in front of him, and he would put his finger on a spot and pray. Then he would spin it, put his finger on another spot, and pray.

Then as F.B. Meyer watched unnoticed, A.B. Simpson leaned forward and took the whole globe in his arms, hugged it, and cried.

Is there built into your heart and lifestyle a genuine, heartfelt reaching out to the world?

+ + +

One of my life purposes is, "Outwardly, to leave a mark on others contemporary to me and following me, through my life and talents, which will point them to God." The reason God leaves us here awhile instead of taking us straight to Heaven is to make a mark on others before we go.

One way you do this is in a small group of peers. The other is by discipling those who haven't walked with

Jesus quite as long as you, and who want to grow. The difference between a peer group and a discipling group is that in discipling, I set the agenda and guide the group along.

I have a section in my notebook called "disciples." At the top of the first page I wrote, "Father, please: one hundred disciples in my lifetime?" In parentheses I put "four a year for twenty-five years?" My list has increased to about eight a year, so I expect, God willing, I can affect hundreds at close range before I die.

What do I do? Each summer, I say to women I feel would be responsive, "What do you say we get together once a week from September to June?" As in any small group, we worship the Lord, we look at the Bible together, we talk about what's going on in our lives, we pray for one another, and in specific ways, we hold one another accountable for growth.

The discipling process ought to be a continual flow through every believer's life—continually learning from someone who knows more than you do, and then (don't be the dead end!) continually passing on what you know to someone who knows less. You say you don't know much? If all you know is John 3:16, get together with somebody who doesn't know John 3:16, have a cup of coffee, and tell that person about it. Then if he says, "Hey, this was great; let's do it again next week," you've got one week to learn something new! Discipling is a stretching occupation![1]

Warm-up
Take five or ten minutes for sharing a life profile and praying.

Scripture Search

1. Read Luke 4:14-21.

    a. What was Jesus' mission, according to 4:18-19?

b. Jesus has passed His mission on to us (John 20:21). How do you think Luke 4:18-19 applies to you?

c. Do you believe you have the power to make this kind of difference in people's lives? Why or why not?

___

2. Take five or ten minutes to make a chart of "evangelistic connections"—people your life touches who don't know the Lord, people to whom you would like to introduce Him. The chart could look like this:

EVANGELISTIC CONNECTIONS				
Family	Neighbors	Friends	Business	Tradespeople
1.	1.	1.	1.	1.
2.	2.	2.	2.	2.
3.	3.	3.	3.	3.

Next to each name, write down at least one need or concern you know the person has. (If you don't know someone well enough to know his needs, there is a project for you.)

3. What keeps you from reaching out to the people you just listed? (Circumstances? Fears? Other attitudes?)

4. Many Christians feel guilty when the topic of evangelism comes up. Why do you suppose this is so?

5. Paul has a lot to say in his second letter to the Corinthians about spreading the news of Christ. Read the following passages: 2 Corinthians 3:4-6, 4:1-12, 5:11-21. As you read, jot down what Paul says about these issues:

   a. What is our mission?

   b. What motivates us to reach out to unbelievers?

   c. What is the solution to our sense of helplessness in the face of so many blind and imprisoned people?

THINK ABOUT IT: Paul says that our weapons to liberate prisoners from Satan are not human, but supernatural (2 Corinthians 10:4). Those weapons are:

▶ the power of the Holy Spirit living in us;
▶ prayer;

▶the Scriptures;
▶love;
▶righteousness living.

You can find these weapons, as well as the armor that protects us in the midst of this battle, in 2 Corinthians 6:3-10 and Ephesians 6:10-18.

Moving Out

In groups of three or four, take ten minutes to pray for the people on your evangelistic connections charts. Take turns naming the people and praying for them and yourselves. Ask God to give you His love for them. Ask Him to begin working in their hearts and drawing them to Himself. Ask Him to direct their circumstances to confront them with their need for Him. Ask Him to make Himself known to them. And finally, ask Him to show you how you can be incarnations of His love and transforming power in their lives.

Commit yourselves to pray for the people on your list every day for the next week. In your daily time with God, read a chapter of 2 Corinthians each day. Keep asking God,

"Who are You, Lord?"
"What should I do, Lord?"

Make plans to telephone one of the members of your group midweek to see how that person is doing. Ask how the time with God is going and whether your friend has had any contact with the nonChristians he put on his list.

NOTE
1. Adapted from Raymond C. Ortlund, *Three Priorities for a Strong Local Church* (Waco, Tex.: Word Books, 1983, 1988), pages 108-110; and Anne Ortlund, *Disciplines of the Beautiful Woman* (Waco, Tex.: Word, Inc., 1977, 1984), pages 85-87.

In Acts chapter eight, we have a big emer-
gency: Philip must minister all by himself!
The problem is quickly rectified (verse 14).
Otherwise the New Testament strategy is
always two by two or in small groups.
                                        —Ray & Anne Ortlund

Teaming Up

Mark 2:1-12 gives us a vivid picture of how the second
priority facilitates the third—how love between believers
helps get new ones to Christ.

Four men carried a paralytic to the Lord Jesus, who
was so surrounded by crowds in a home that they had to
let the cripple down through the roof, and Jesus healed
him.

Notice how *teamwork among believers brings*
people to Jesus. There lay a man—paralyzed physically,
just as unbelievers in your community are paralyzed
morally and spiritually. These four believers in Jesus
cooperated to bring this man to Him, when he couldn't
get there on his own.

Christians stimulate each other. They are willing to
do with others what they'd never attempt alone. A fellow
in a small group with me once said about this passage,
"I'd be the fourth man here who put his hand to the
stretcher. I'm not the kind who leads boldly in initiating
things, but I sure love to be with guys who do!"

One man in this story had to get the idea: "Fellows,
there's poor old Joe over there. The only one who can heal
him is Jesus. Why don't we carry him to Jesus together?"
So he enlisted the other three.

65

It took unity to get him there—but unity is costly. Cooperating means submission, sometimes swallowing your opinions; it means fitting in with the rest; it means love in action. People can be great individualists: "No one's going to tell me what to do!" This spirit can keep Christians from helping paralyzed people get to Christ. Isolated believers just aren't attractive.

Loving people to Christ calls for teamwork! How Jesus and His disciples worked together! He sent out His disciples two by two. Paul and company went everywhere together. Today, small Bible study groups—supporting one another and praying for one another as they seek to love that one or this one—can be most effective in reaching our neighborhood-world for Christ.

When the people heard that Jesus had come home, "So many gathered that there was no room left, not even outside the door, and he preached the word to them" (Mark 2:2). To go with Christ is costly. Where Jesus is, needy people keep coming, jostling, pressing in on the situation. There's confusion, there's the draining of emotions. It's costly to get into the business of loving, helping, restoring, healing, and caring!

But the effect on the world may be powerful. Jesus prayed later "that all of [my followers] may be one, Father . . . *that the world may believe.*" Then He went on to pray, "May they be brought to complete unity *to let the world know*" (John 17:21,23; emphasis added). Christian unity brings people to the Lord Jesus! And Jesus had already told the disciples, "*All men will know* that you are my disciples, if you love one another" (John 13:35, emphasis added).

Small groups are perfect little laboratories for testing and proving that Christian unity brings people to Jesus. For quite a while, Anne and I were in a group with four other couples who met each Thursday evening of the month, except the third Thursday when the group hosted a special Bible study for our unsaved friends. We met in various living rooms, put out a spread of refreshments as "bait," and conducted a low-key, hang-loose discussion of some evangelistic passage of Scripture. Loving cooperation and lots of prayer behind the scenes on the part of those couples proved that God's principle works. Dozens of friends came to accept Christ in that Bible study!

Another lesson I see in Mark 2:1-12 is, *faith brings people to Jesus.* Verse 5 says, "When Jesus saw their faith, he said to the paralytic, 'Son, your sins are forgiven.'"

Whose faith? *Their* faith. This story doesn't exclude the faith of the paralytic, but it concentrates on the faith of the four who brought him. *They believed Jesus would use their efforts.* And that made carrying the dead weight of a grown man through the streets and up the stairs and through a hole in the roof—all that—worth it.

Others were perhaps saying, "What a sideshow!" Faith acts. Unbelief only reacts.

Many Christians haven't led anyone to Christ— ever—or not for so many years that they really don't think God would ever use them in that way! To overcome their dullness, their lack of hope—to build faith—they need to team up with believers who believe!

> You'll do more
>   When you're four
> Than you've ever done
>   When you're one!

The story ends with everyone around Jesus being amazed. And that's what life in the church will be when brothers and sisters in Christ believe deeply in the power of their common Lord as their first priority, when they commit to live and love together as their second priority, and when they move out in unity and faith to the needy world around them as their third priority.[1]

Warm-up

Let someone share his or her life profile, then pray for that person.

1. Ray names several advantages of teaming up with other Christians to spread the gospel. What are the advantages? (Add any you can think of yourself.)

2. What are the risks and costs of teaming up?

3. Discuss all the reasons why you are reluctant to get involved with unbelievers. (Be honest!)

Moving Out

Spend the rest of your meeting strategizing how to reach the people you listed during the last session. Begin with five or ten minutes of prayer, asking God to work in those people's lives and to show you what He wants you to do. Then make some specific plans. (A dinner party? A cookout? Going jogging with your neighbor? An evangelistic Bible study like the one Ray describes?) Use your ingenuity!

Remember: Jesus says that loving and being one with other Christians will draw unbelievers to Him (John 13:35, 17:21-23).

Other Voices

Most people admire philanthropy, missions, and witnessing—but they leave them to the super people on whom they look with not a little awe and reverence. That's ridiculous! There are people all around us in deep trouble and desperately floundering, and they would welcome us as angels if we lent them some money, told them about Jesus, or met whatever their need happens to be.

We know this, but why don't we act? Because if you're like me, I'm naturally—well, "chicken" is the word. I need a group of Christians to whom I'm regularly accountable, to whom I can lay out the needs of those around me, and who will be responsible for seeing that I act.

One day in the beauty parlor I sat down as usual under the hair dryer and was approached by a cute redhead.

"Hi," she said, "I'm Barbara. Your manicurist quit last week, and I'm taking over her patrons."

"Hello, Barbara," I said, and five minutes later she was sharing that her husband had left her, that she was afraid of being at home alone at night, that the children all thought it was her fault and not his—soon tears were falling all over my nail polish.

[I invited Barbara to come to Sunday school and church with me, and to hang around afterward.] Through the following weeks Barbara came with me, and there was also an invisible foundation being laid that she knew nothing about. Every week my group of sisters would ask, "What can we pray for, for Barbara? What's happening in your relationship with her? Who can take Barbara out for a meal? Who is talking with her about the Lord?" And then they'd pray—for me, for our group effort, and for Barbara.

Well, that kind of prodding from the rear is what any Christian needs who doesn't naturally have the gift of evangelism. No wonder Barbara soon came to know the Lord![2]

—Anne Ortlund

NOTES
1. Adapated from Raymond C. Ortlund, *Three Priorities for a Strong Local Church* (Waco, Tex.: Word Books, 1983, 1988), pages 93-98.
2. Anne Ortlund, *Disciplines of the Beautiful Woman* (Waco, Tex.: Word, Inc., 1977, 1984), pages 33-34.

Living the
Three Priorities

*If you have to ask how to do it, you ain't
got it.*

         —*Louis (Satchmo) Armstrong*

Living in Liberty

Toad baked some cookies. "These cookies smell very good," said Toad. He ate one. "And they taste even better," he said. Toad ran to Frog's house. "Frog, Frog," cried Toad, "taste these cookies that I have made."

Frog ate one of the cookies, "These are the best cookies I have ever eaten!" said Frog.

Frog and Toad ate many cookies, one after another. "You know, Toad," said Frog, with his mouth full, "I think we should stop eating. We will soon be sick."

"You are right," said Toad. "Let us eat one last cookie, and then we will stop." Frog and Toad ate one last cookie. There were many cookies left in the bowl.

"Frog," said Toad, "let us eat one very last cookie, and then we will stop." Frog and Toad ate one very last cookie.

"We must stop eating!" cried Toad as he ate another.

"Yes," said Frog, reaching for a cookie, "we need willpower."

"What is willpower?" asked Toad.

"Willpower is trying hard not to do something you really want to do," said Frog.

"You mean like trying hard not to eat all these cookies?" asked Toad.

"Right," said Frog.

Frog put the cookies in a box. "There," he said. "Now we will not eat any more cookies."

"But we can open the box," said Toad.

"That is true," said Frog.

Frog tied some string around the box. "There," he said. "Now we will not eat any more cookies."

"But we can cut the string and open the box," said Toad.

"That is true," said Frog.

Frog got a ladder. He put the box up on a high shelf. "There," said Frog. "Now we will not eat any more cookies."

"But we can climb the ladder and take the box down from the shelf and cut the string and open the box," said Toad.

"That is true," said Frog.

Frog climbed the ladder and took the box down from the shelf. He cut the string and opened the box.

Frog took the box outside. He shouted in a loud voice. "Hey, birds, here are cookies!" Birds came from everywhere. They picked up all the cookies in their beaks and flew away.

"Now we have no more cookies to eat," said Toad sadly. "Not even one."

"Yes," said Frog, "but we have lots and lots of willpower."

"You may keep it all, Frog," said Toad. "I am going home now to bake a cake."[1]

Toad is obviously not liberated. He's chained to his love of cookies, as you are chained to your love of _____ . (You can fill in the blank.)

We're all chained to lots of things. They get in the way of our putting Christ first and committing ourselves to the Body of Christ and to the world. What does Romans 7 say about this? It says:

The Christian life isn't hard; it's impossible.

Face it: you can't live the Christian life. If you're trying to live by the three priorities in your own strength, you're already worried and uptight.

Sometimes people say, "Well, I believe that if a person believes in Christ and does the best he can, he'll be all right." That may sound good, but it doesn't work. Because no one ever does the best he can.

Do you?

Have you done the very best you could for the past seven weeks at loving the Lord, loving fellow Christians, and loving this needy world—all in fresh measurable ways? What about for the past seven days? Even for the past day?

So Romans 3:23 says, "All have sinned and fall short of the glory of God." You just can't get up there to God's glory by your own efforts.[2]

Warm-up
Finish your last life profile, and take time to pray for the person sharing it.

Scripture Search

1. Read Romans 7:7-25. (Hang in there; it's a tough passage.) From what Paul says, do you agree or disagree that "the Christian life isn't hard; it's impossible"? Why?

2. To what extent has your own experience of trying to live by the three priorities been like what Paul describes? Give some examples.

3. Read Romans 8:1-17.

a. According to Paul, how should we go about trying to live by the three priorities? Explain these statements in your own words:

▶ "There is now no condemnation for those who are in Christ Jesus" (8:1).
▶ "Through Christ Jesus the law of the Spirit of life set me free from the law of sin and death" (8:2).
▶ "Those who live in accordance with the Spirit have their minds set on what the Spirit desires" (8:5).
▶ "By the Spirit . . . put to death the misdeeds of the body" (8:13).

b. What do you think it means in practical terms to live according to the Spirit? (Give examples from your own life.)

c. Have you been trying to approach the three priorities in this way? If so, how has it gone? What successes and/or frustrations have you experienced?

d. Whether or not you've tried the Romans 8 approach, what questions do you have about how it works?

e. What potential difficulties do you foresee in the Romans 8 approach, if any?

THINK ABOUT IT: Do you think it is possible to live according to the Spirit without practicing God's presence and spending daily time alone with Him? Why or why not?

Paul explains more of what he means by living according to the Spirit in Romans 8:13-16; 2 Corinthians 4:7-18; and Ephesians 3:1-6, 5:1-21.

4. James Ryle defines grace as "the empowering presence of God to cause you to be who God made you to be and to do what God calls you to do."

With this definition in mind, what does it mean to say that God's "grace is sufficient for you, for [God's] power is made perfect in weakness" (2 Corinthians 12:9)?

5. How can you approach the three priorities "according to the Spirit" and grace rather than according to self-effort and willpower? (Be as specific and practical in your answer as you can.)

Moving Out

Divide into pairs. Take five or ten minutes to tell God about how you feel you are doing at living by the three priorities—which of the three you're weak in, and where you're strong. Tell Him your fears, but also your dreams and specific ideas for strengthening where you're weak.

Then ask God to provide your prayer partner with the grace—His empowering presence—he or she needs to live committed to Christ, to His Body, and to the world. Let your prayers be guided by the thoughts and feelings your partner has expressed.

Pray for grace for yourself and your prayer partner this week during your times alone with God. Ask Him to provide you with the strength to stay committed to godly priorities for your life. For the battles of your daily life, consciously draw on the grace He provides through the Scriptures, prayer, and relationship with other Christians. Telephone your partner midweek to see how he or she is doing at living by grace, and to pray for each other.

NOTES
1. Arnold Lobel, *Frog and Toad Together* (New York: Harper and Row, 1972).
2. Adapted from Raymond C. Ortlund, *Be a New Christian All Your Life* (Old Tappan, N.J.: Fleming H. Revell, 1983), pages 43-45.

Don't let these sessions be just an event,
but the beginning of a process.
                        —Ray & Anne Ortlund

Where to From Here?

We said at the beginning that the purpose of this guide is not
to study renewal, but to be renewed. Our hope is that the
three priorities won't be just a topic you've studied for a few
weeks, but a way of life from now on. That's what renewal is—
seeing new areas of obedience and stepping out, relying on
God's Holy Spirit to enable you.

So, we strongly suggest that you spend another meeting
taking stock as a group and asking yourselves, "Now what?"
Here are some possible questions you can discuss:

---

1. a. How has the attempt to put Christ at the center of your
   lives affected you . . .

   as individuals?

   as a group?

as families?

b. How can you keep putting Christ first as an individual, as a group, and as a family?
    In groups of three or four, brainstorm some practical strategies. (Don't forget to rely on grace, not self-effort.)

2. a. How have you done at caring for each other? (Try to be honest with each other.)

b. How can you do better in this area?

3. a. What has been tough about reaching out to unbelievers?

b. How can you continue to reach out to unbelievers?

WHERE TO FROM HERE?   83

4. a. What have you learned about relying on God's power
rather than your own?

b. How can this affect the way you approach the priorities
from now on?

5. a. In sessions 1 and 4, you set some goals for yourselves. How
well have you accomplished them?

b. To what extent do you still think they are valid goals?

c. How would you like to extend or in some other way
change those goals for the future?

Here are some suggestions for going on with the priorities as a
group, or as individuals until you're involved in other groups.
      First, keep in touch with one member of your group. Tele-
phone each other once a week to discuss how quiet times with
God are going, what He's teaching you, and how you can pray
for each other. Keep sharing your schedules and goals.
      Next, plan with three other members of your group to
meet once a month specifically to pray for unbelievers in your
lives and to plan ways to reach out to them. You might invite
several nonChristian singles and/or couples to join you for a

buffet dinner and an open discussion of a topic, such as raising children, relationships, or "What if there's a God?"

Set aside fifteen minutes every fourth meeting of your group to share how you are doing at putting Christ at the center of your lives. You could have a couple of group members tell how it's going, then pray together for the grace to continue choosing this difficult but crucial priority.

Finally, maintain space at each meeting to hear and pray about each other's concerns. Look for ways to carry one another's burdens.

+ + +

The goal of these nine sessions is true renewal of your life. Read out loud this last page of Ray's book, *Lord, Make My Life A Miracle*, and then allow enough closing time for leisurely prayer as a group, perhaps on your knees:

What are you going to quit in life to get these priorities accomplished?
Your danger and mine is not that we become criminals, but rather that we become respectable, decent, commonplace, mediocre Christians. The twentieth-century temptations that really sap our spiritual power are the television, banana cream pie, the easy chair, and the credit card. The Christian wins or loses in those seemingly innocent little moments of decision.
Lord, make my life a miracle![1]

NOTE
1. Raymond C. Ortlund, *Lord, Make My Life a Miracle* (Ventura, Calif.: Regal Books, 1974), page 151.